TREASURE

SHIPWRECKS

NICK HUNTER

Raintree

Chicago, Illinois

Edited by Laura Knowles, Adam Miller,
Harriet Milles, and Helen Cox Cannons
Designed by Victoria Allen
Original illustrations © Capstone Global Library
Ltd 2013
Illustrated by Martin Bustamante
Picture research by Tracy Cummins

Originated by Capstone Global Library Ltd
Production by Alison Parsons

**Library of Congress Cataloging-in-Publication
Data**
Hunter, Nick.

  Shipwrecks / Nick Hunter.—1st ed.
     p. cm.—(Treasure hunters)
  Includes bibliographical references and index.
  ISBN 978-1-4109-4954-7 (hbk.)—ISBN 978-1-
4109-4961-5 (pbk.) 1. Shipwrecks—Juvenile
literature. 2. Treasure troves—Juvenile literature.
I. Title.
  G525.H8976 2013
  910.4′52—dc23   2012012892

Acknowledgments
We would like to thank the following for
permission to reproduce photos: Alamy 7 (©Mary
Evans Picture Library), 12 (©Roger Bamber), 13
(©Terry Fincher, Photo Int), 14t (©UK History),
37 (©celebrity); ©AP Photo 35; Art Resources
34 (©20th Century Fox/Paramount/The Kobal
Collection/Wallace, Merie W.); Bridgeman Art
Library 9 (©Basire, James/Private Collection);
Corbis 14b (©Adam Woolfitt), 17 (©The Gallery
Collection), 19 (©Derek Bayes-Art/Lebrecht Music
& Arts), 23 (©Jonathan Blair), 33, 36 (©Ralph
White), 43 (© Stephen Frink); Getty Images 15
(©RDImages/Epics), 31 (©National Geographic),
39 (©Michel Boutefeu); Istockphoto 20 (©
Sharon Metson); ©Library of Congress Prints

and Photographs 6, 27; Newscom 8, 30 (©ZUMA
Press), 16 (©HANA KALVACHOV/ISIFA/SIPA), 22b
(©David Spencer/Palm Beach Post /ZUMA Press),
25 (©AFP/GETTY IMAGES), 29t (©EMMANUEL
DUNAND/AFP/Getty Images); NOAA 29b
(©side-scan-sonar-rude), 38 (©OAR/National
Undersea Research Program (NURP); Woods
Hole Oceanographic Inst.); Press Association
Images 5b (©Chris Ison/PA Archive); Shutterstock
1 (©bioraven), 4t (©EpicStockMedia), 5t (©ded
pixto), 8t (©Alex Staroseltsev), 10 (©James Steidl),
18 (©Larry Jacobsen), 21 (©frantisekhojdysz), 22t
(©Rashevskyi Viacheslav), 26 (©Nejron Photo),
28b (©ID1974), 28t (©Rich Carey), 32t (©Sergej
Khakimullin); Superstock p.32b (©Titanic Images/
Universal Images Group); The Image Works 4b, 11
(©National Maritime Museum, London). Design
features: ©Shutterstock.

Cover photos reproduced with permission of
istockphoto (©EXTREME-PHOTOGRAPHER) and
Getty Images (©Reinhard Dirscherl).

Expert consultant
We would like to thank Dr. Linda
Hulin for her invaluable help in the
preparation of this book. Dr. Hulin
is research assistant to the director
at the Oxford Center for Maritime
Archaeology, University of Oxford,
England, and director of the Western
Marmarica Coastal Survey, Libya.

Guided Reading Level: U

CONTENTS

TREASURE BENEATH THE WAVES

Newspapers broke the news across Europe. A storm had claimed the *Merchant Royal*, which had taken its precious cargo of gold and silver to the seabed close to Land's End, at the southwestern tip of England. The loss of the *Merchant Royal* and its treasure in 1641 meant ruin for merchants and bankers. But for treasure hunters everywhere, the ship's fate meant that there was fabulous treasure lying somewhere beneath the English Channel, just waiting to be discovered.

A fleet of English merchant ships sail through a storm. The *Merchant Royal* would have looked like this.

The search for the *Merchant Royal*'s treasure continues to this day. The latest technology, including diving equipment and submarines, has made it easier for treasure hunters to find riches beneath the waves, but there are still many shipwrecks that have not been discovered.

WINDOWS ON THE PAST

For thousands of years, ships were the only way for people and goods to travel across seas and oceans. Often these voyages ended in a shipwreck. Sinking ships took treasures with them to the seabed. But treasure hunters can discover more than just riches. Wrecks of ships, such as the Civil War-era SS *Republic*, can give us a window into the lives of the people who sailed them, through the everyday items they left behind.

Shipwrecks are incredibly fragile. It is important that they are explored by trained archaeologists, so that we can learn as much as possible about them and preserve them for the future.

The *Merchant Royal* was carrying one of the richest cargoes ever lost at sea, including more than 500,000 Spanish silver coins and 500 gold ingots.

WHAT CAUSES SHIPWRECKS?

Ships can be wrecked for many different reasons. The immense power of ocean storms can drive even the biggest ships onto rocky coasts. In the past, wooden ships like the *Merchant Royal* could be torn apart by wind and waves.

During centuries of warfare, warships have tried to sink their enemies with cannons and artillery. Torpedoes fired from submarines were used to sink warships and cargo vessels, such as the British passenger liner *Lusitania*.

Other shipwrecks happen because of freak accidents or collisions. Although shipwrecks can contain treasures for explorers and archaeologists, people must always remember that a wreck may have claimed the lives of many people.

Almost 1,200 people died when the *Lusitania* was sunk by a German torpedo in 1915. Many people think the huge loss of life was partly because the ship was secretly carrying some explosives.

Exploring underwater

To discover and recover treasures beneath the sea, people have to be able to breathe underwater. Even thousands of years ago, divers would carry a supply of air in a barrel. Today, treasure hunters can use manned and unmanned submarines to explore many miles below the surface.

There are an amazing three million wrecks beneath the world's oceans. Many of these are undiscovered and could hold exciting secrets and treasure from the past.

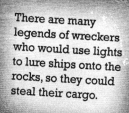

There are many legends of wreckers who would use lights to lure ships onto the rocks, so they could steal their cargo.

THE MARY ROSE

England is under attack. It is July 1545, and a French fleet of more than 200 ships is approaching the south coast. King Henry VIII of England watches anxiously from the shore as his smaller fleet sails out to do battle with his enemies. His favorite ship, the *Mary Rose*, leads the way.

Even if they could have escaped from a ship, many sailors could not swim in the 1500s. They believed that learning to swim would bring bad luck and their ship would surely sink.

The *Mary Rose* was one of the greatest ships of its time.

DISASTER STRIKES

As it nears the French ships, the *Mary Rose* turns to point its cannons at the enemy. A sudden gust of wind catches the ship, pushing it onto one side. As water fills its lowest gun ports, the ship cannot recover. The *Mary Rose* sinks in minutes.

Around 500 men were drowned as the ship sank beneath the waves. The ship's decks were protected by nets to stop the enemy from boarding. These nets stopped the crew from escaping the sinking ship.

In this picture of the battle, the *Mary Rose's* masts can just be seen poking out of the water.

HOW DID IT HAPPEN?

From the moment the *Mary Rose* disappeared beneath the waves, people asked why the disaster had happened. At first, the French claimed that their guns had damaged the *Mary Rose*. The real reason was a dangerous mix of the ship's design and mistakes made by its crew. Most of the crew members paid for these mistakes with their lives.

Carrying heavy cannons and lots of extra people to fire them made the *Mary Rose* difficult for the crew to manage.

"... WHEN SHE HEELED [TILTED] OVER WITH THE WIND THE WATER ENTERED BY THE LOWEST ROW OF GUN PORTS WHICH HAD BEEN LEFT OPEN AFTER FIRING."

A REPORT FROM A SURVIVOR OF THE DISASTER

The ship had been part of Henry VIII's navy for more than 30 years. It had been refitted with more cannons to smash the sides of enemy ships. These cannons probably played a part in the sinking of the *Mary Rose* itself.

If a ship's gun ports were too high above the water, the heavy cannons would overbalance the ship. Gun ports had to be close to the waterline, and the crew members had to make sure they were closed when the ship was moving. Eyewitness reports say that this did not happen. When the ship was tilted over by a gust of wind, it filled with water and was doomed.

GEORGE CAREW

Born: c. 1504

Died: 1545

Nationality: British

Vice-admiral and captain of the Mary Rose, *Carew was one of the hundreds who died on the ship. Carew was in charge of all aspects of life on board ship. He described his own crew as "the sort of knaves whom he could not rule."*

Mary Rose

FINDING THE WRECK

Over hundreds of years, the ship sank into the sand on the seabed. Currents and marine creatures ate away at the timbers that were above the sand.

In 1836, a fisherman's net became caught on an object on the seabed. Diver John Deane was brought in to free the net and was amazed to discover that it was caught on the remains of the famous warship. He salvaged a cannon that proved the wreck was the *Mary Rose*. After a few dives, the wreck was forgotten again.

In the 1960s, Alexander McKee had a hunch that he could find the ship. People said his team was crazy as they used sonar to scan the seabed for the ship. Was the large object they found covered in mud on the seabed a 400-year-old warship? If so, they had to remove the mud and sand incredibly gently so they did not damage the ancient timbers. Slowly, the timbers of the *Mary Rose* began to emerge.

This diver is getting ready to dive down to the *Mary Rose*.

RAISING THE MARY ROSE

Finding the ship was one thing, but lifting it back to the surface of the sea was a huge project. First, the *Mary Rose* had to be lifted out of the seabed inch by inch, so it could be moved to a supporting cradle. Finally, on October 11, 1982, the *Mary Rose* was lifted clear of the water by a massive floating crane.

After 400 years underwater, the *Mary Rose* is lifted from the seabed.

13

ALEXANDER MCKEE

Born: 1918

Died: 1992

Nationality: British

He was the man behind the project to find and raise the *Mary Rose*. McKee made the first dive to the wreck site in 1966. It took five years for his team to be sure that the wreck was the *Mary Rose*—but even then they did not know about the amazing treasures inside.

FASCINATING FINDS

The treasure of the *Mary Rose* was not gold or silver, but rather what the ship itself and the many things it contained could tell us about life at sea 500 years ago. In addition to cannons and other weapons, the wreck's contents included clothing, food, and musical instruments. Archaeologists also have the gruesome task of studying the skeletons of the *Mary Rose*'s crew and even the bones of the rats that went down with the ship.

Finds from the ship included this board game.

Preserving the ship

The battle to preserve the ship never stops. For more than 20 years after it was raised from the seabed, the ship's timbers were sprayed with water and later a waxy material. This stopped the ancient wood from decaying and breaking apart as it dried out. More than 20,000 precious historical artifacts from the ship also need to be preserved.

Live pond snails were used to protect some items from the ship. They ate fungi and other organisms that would attack the delicate objects.

Preserved Mary Rose

Sterncastle

Keelson

TREASURE FLEET TRAGEDY

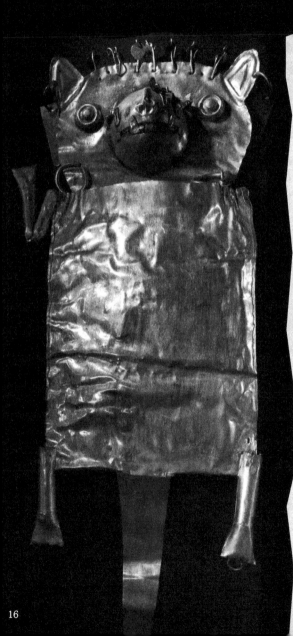

One of the greatest and most destructive treasure hunts of all was the Spanish search for gold and silver in the "New World" of Central and South America. Following in the footsteps of Christopher Columbus, Spanish explorers such as Hernán Cortés looted the treasure of the Aztec and Inca civilizations to provide riches for Spain.

Every summer, two fleets of ships would leave the Caribbean carrying this treasure. It was a risky journey, as they dodged pirates and the hurricanes that usually hit the region from late July onward.

In 1622, a treasure fleet left Havana, Cuba, on September 4. It was running late, and the hurricane season was starting. The richest treasure was carried by the heavily armed *Nuestra Señora de Atocha*, at the back of the fleet.

Beautiful gold ornaments were melted down to make money for the Spanish.

Navigation

Ships of the 1600s did not have the accurate navigation and weather information of today's ocean-going vessels. Captains could use the position of the Sun to tell how far north or south they were, but it was much more difficult to know their position east or west. Whenever possible, they followed the coast, risking a wreck on rocky shores.

The *Atocha* was carrying an amazing cargo including 35 tons of silver, more than 100 gold ingots, jewels, and other precious metals.

Galleons crossing the Atlantic Ocean sailed together to avoid being picked off by pirates.

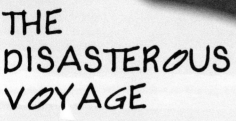

THE DISASTEROUS VOYAGE

Just a day after leaving Havana, a fierce hurricane hit the treasure fleet. The ships at the rear, including the *Atocha*, became separated from the rest by the howling winds and mountainous waves. The ship, loaded down with its treasure, was driven onto a coral reef off the coast of Florida and sank in shallow coastal waters.

Of the 265 people on board, just three crew members and two slaves survived by clinging to the ship's mast. A passing merchant ship rescued them and tried to get into the *Atocha*, but its hatches were tightly closed. With no diving equipment, they could only work underwater for a very short time.

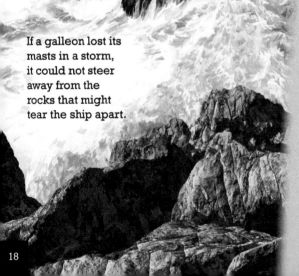

If a galleon lost its masts in a storm, it could not steer away from the rocks that might tear the ship apart.

"... SUDDENLY THEY CAME TO SHALLOW WATER, AND IN SHORT SPACE RAN HERSELF ON GROUND ... WITH THE LOSS OF HER PEOPLE, EXCEPT THREE MEN AND TWO BOYS: THIS WAS ON THE COAST OF MARACAMBE IN FLORIDA."

FROM AN ENGLISH ACCOUNT OF THE SHIPWRECK OF THE ATOCHA, 1623

STILL NO LUCK

Spanish salvagers tried for many years to get their hands on the sunken treasure. Storms and waves moved the ship and, in the end, they had to give up. It seemed as if the *Atocha*'s riches would remain out of reach.

There was so much treasure lost with the *Atocha* that the Spanish government had to borrow more money to finance its wars.

Galleons like this one were designed to carry treasure and up to 60 cannons.

crew's quarters

hold for treasure

captain's and officers' cabins

cannons for protection

Even with the latest equipment, exploring shipwrecks on the seabed still carries many dangers.

THE SEARCH FOR THE ATOCHA

The lure of the *Atocha*'s fabulous treasure did not die. Historical records told the story of the wreck and its precious cargo. In the 1960s, the treasure hunter Mel Fisher began to follow the trail of the galleon.

The search was a long one. For many years, Fisher and his team found objects and clues that showed a wreck was nearby, but they could not tell if it was the *Atocha*. The first breakthrough came in 1973. Three silver ingots were found that matched the list of treasure carried by the missing galleon.

DIVING DISASTER

In 1975, disaster struck the salvage team. Fisher's son Dirk had just found some cannons that proved the *Atocha* was nearby when a dive boat turned over, killing Dirk, his wife, and another diver. The tragic accident spurred Fisher on to complete the job and find the treasure.

Diving technology

The search for the *Atocha* could never have happened without the invention of SCUBA diving. In 1942, Jacques-Yves Cousteau developed the Aqua-Lung. This metal container filled with air helped divers to stay underwater for longer and to move freely without being attached to an air supply on the surface.

MEL FISHER

Born: 1922

Died: 1998

Nationality: American

Mel Fisher made his first diving helmet out of a bucket, a piece of hose, and a bicycle pump. He went on to become one of the world's most successful treasure hunters, beginning with the search for a Spanish treasure fleet that was wrecked in 1715. The 16-year search for the Atocha was his greatest triumph.

THE MOTHER LODE

The motto of the team searching for the *Atocha* was "Today's the day." For every day when they made a major discovery, there were hundreds when their search for treasure seemed useless. But on July 20, 1985, two divers were amazed to discover a huge pile of more than 1,000 silver bars beneath the ocean.

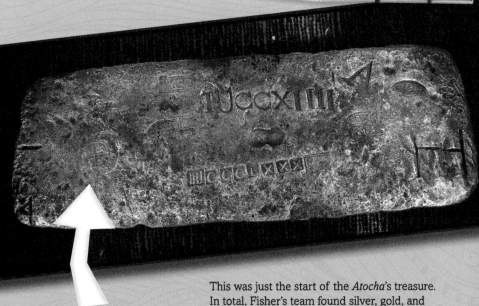

This is a silver ingot from *Nuestra Señora de Atocha.*

This was just the start of the *Atocha*'s treasure. In total, Fisher's team found silver, gold, and jewels valued at up to $400 million. In addition to this treasure, there were priceless artifacts of the region's colonial history.

> "I STILL RECALL MY FIRST DIVE ON THE ATOCHA SITE VIVIDLY. IT WAS LIKE BEING TRANSPORTED BACK IN TIME, OVER 350 YEARS, TO THE DAY THIS HISTORIC SHIP WENT DOWN ... SILVER COINS, BITS OF POTTERY, AND SWORDS WERE CLEARLY VISIBLE TO THE TRAINED EYE."
>
> **R. DUNCAN MATHEWSON III, ARCHAEOLOGIST**

CONTROVERSY

Governments and archaeologists accuse treasure hunters like Mel Fisher of being more interested in making money than in preserving historic sites. They argue that treasure hunters disturb historic sites. The whole shipwreck is important, not just the treasures it may hold. The International Convention on Underwater Cultural Heritage was introduced to help prevent wrecks and treasure from being salvaged for profit.

Professional treasure hunters point out that they spend many years and lots of money finding some of history's most important shipwrecks. Others argue cultural heritage belongs to everybody and should not be sold to the highest bidder.

Mel Fisher's search for treasure made him a controversial figure.

SS REPUBLIC

The crippled paddle steamer had been battling a hurricane for two days. Howling winds and huge waves had flooded the ship's boilers and left it drifting without power in the ferocious storm. The reserve boiler that powered the pumps had also been swamped. Without these pumps, the crew and passengers knew the ship was sinking. They were around 100 miles (160 kilometers) from the coast of Georgia.

Much of the SS *Republic's* cargo had already been thrown overboard, apart from the barrels of gold coins and other treasure that they were carrying. People feverishly bailed buckets of water from the hold to buy a bit of time until the lifeboats were ready.

At 4:00 p.m. on October 25, 1865, the SS *Republic* finally sank to the bottom of the ocean. Amazingly, all the crew and passengers managed to scramble into the lifeboats, although they still had to survive the storm for two days or more, until they could be rescued by passing ships.

> "IT WAS DESPERATION INTENSIFIED. NO MAN STOPPED TO THINK WHAT WAS THE FATE IMPENDING IN A FEW HOURS, AND YET BUT FEW HOPED FOR ANYTHING BUT LIFE, AND NONE EXPECTED ANYTHING BUT DEATH."

FROM AN ACCOUNT BY COLONEL WILLIAM NICHOLS, A PASSENGER, ON THE DESPERATE BATTLE TO SAVE THE SS *REPUBLIC*

COLONEL WILLIAM NICHOLS

Born: 1829

Died: 1882

Nationality: American

William Nichols had already lived through the battles of the Civil War. He survived many days in an open boat after the sinking of the SS Republic. Nichols described his ordeal in a letter to his wife, without knowing that she was dying of typhoid fever.

the SS *Republic*

SURVIVAL

The last survivors of the SS *Republic* were picked up on November 2, a week after the disaster. Two men were found clinging to a raft. Fourteen of their companions had been washed away or jumped from the raft and were never seen again. Amazingly, most of the ship's 80 passengers and crew lived to tell the tale.

> "OUR THROATS BEGAN TO SWELL FROM THIRST ... AT THIS POINT WE WERE ON THE POINT OF DESPAIR, AND TOOK OFF OUR CLOTHING AND JUMPED INTO THE SEA, TO ABSORB MOISTURE EXTERNALLY, WHICH ALLEVIATED OUR SUFFERING VERY MUCH FOR THE TIME BEING."

THE PASSENGERS' SUFFERING DID NOT END WHEN THE SS REPUBLIC SANK, AS REPORTED BY WILLIAM NICHOLS

The SS *Republic* had already survived three hurricanes before disaster struck on its voyage to New Orleans.

A DISTINGUISHED CAREER

The SS *Republic* itself was a war veteran and had been used as a warship by both sides during the Civil War. The ship had survived many years of war and extreme weather before meeting the "perfect storm" in 1865.

The ship was headed for New Orleans, carrying everything—from cloth to harmonicas—that was in short supply in the southern states following the Civil War. It was also carrying gold and silver coins, worth more than $300,000 at the time. As the ship sank in the deep ocean, it seemed as if the treasure would be lost forever.

The SS *Republic*'s final voyage was an essential mission to help rebuild the southern states ravaged by the Civil War.

DEEP-SEA SEARCH

For more than 100 years after the sinking of the SS *Republic*, the wreck was too deep and far from the coast to be reached by divers. But modern search-and-recovery technology brought the treasure within reach.

In 2002 and 2003, Odyssey Marine Exploration studied newspaper articles from the time, survivors' reports, and computer models of the ship's journey to try to locate the wreck. It used sonar to scan more than 1,500 square miles (3,885 square kilometers) of ocean as well as magnetometers that could detect metals on the seabed.

AN EXCITING FIND!

The team used an unmanned submarine called an ROV (remotely operated vehicle) to study the many wrecks found by the sonar survey. It found a wreck with two large paddle wheels that matched the size of the *Republic*. Was it the ship they were all looking for, revealed after 140 years?

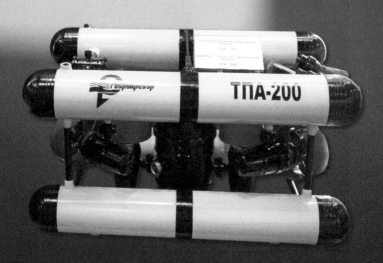

GREG STEMM

Born: 1957

Nationality: American

Greg Stemm is the cofounder of Odyssey Marine Exploration, which has also found the shipwrecks HMS Sussex and HMS Victory. He is a pioneer of wreck investigation using technology rather than divers. He aims to find treasure without putting his team in danger, possibly because, as a child, Stemm lost his grandfather in a marine accident and only just survived himself.

Sonar

Sonar technology uses sound waves to map and locate underwater objects. Sound waves are emitted into the water below a ship. These echo off the seabed or other objects and are picked up by receivers. The first sonar systems were developed during World War I (1914–1918) to detect enemy submarines. Modern systems use computers to create detailed maps of the seabed.

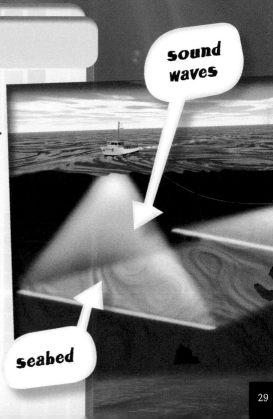

sound waves

seabed

RECLAIMING THE GOLD

These are gold coins from the SS *Republic*. The wreck was in international territory, so no government could claim the treasure as its own property.

Although the wreck seemed to be a paddle steamer from the right time period, the treasure hunters had to be sure. In the fall of 2003, they found a corroded ship's bell. They were able to make out part of the word "Tennessee," which was the original name of the *Republic*. Now, where was the treasure?

Finding the wreck was one thing, but reclaiming the treasure was another challenge. The wreck was found 100 miles (160 kilometers) off Savannah, Georgia, at a depth of 1,700 feet (500 meters). Then, on November 5, 2003, the Odyssey team discovered a coin poking out of the sand at the back of the ship. This was the first sign of an unbelievable treasure and many other priceless artifacts detailing the history of the time.

Estimates put the value of the 51,000 gold and silver coins found on the *Republic* at up to $180 million.

The *Republic's* cargo included a collection of more than 6,000 glass and stoneware bottles, which gave a fascinating picture of Civil War life. Their contents ranged from ink to medicines that promised to cure every known disease.

Robot recovery

The Zeus ROV that was used to excavate the wreck weighed around 7 tons and was the size of a tank. It needed to be big to fight the strong ocean currents and stay in position. Zeus could transmit video of the wreck and lift heavy objects, but it could also recover delicate artifacts and coins.

remote control

DISCOVERY
BALTIMORE. MD.

ROV

THE "UNSINKABLE" TITANIC

The RMS *Titanic* is probably the most famous shipwreck in history. In 1912, huge ocean liners were the only way for passengers to cross the oceans. The *Titanic* was supposed to be "practically unsinkable," with 16 watertight compartments inside its hull, meaning that it would still float even if up to four sections were damaged.

The majestic ship nearly collided with another ship as it left for its maiden voyage from Southampton, England, on April 10, 1912. Some passengers saw this as a sign of bad luck. After this close shave, the voyage went smoothly until the night of April 14.

On that night, despite receiving several warnings of icebergs in the area, the *Titanic* steamed on toward New York. Then, at 11:40 p.m., lookouts spotted a huge iceberg dead ahead. The crew was relieved when the iceberg just scraped the side of the *Titanic*. But as reports came in of water in several of the ship's compartments, Captain Edward Smith knew that the ship was facing disaster.

CAPTAIN EDWARD SMITH

Born: 1850

Died: 1912

Nationality: British

The captain of the *Titanic* died when the ship sank on April 15, 1912. Smith was the White Star Line's most experienced captain, and the *Titanic*'s maiden voyage was supposed to be his last command before retiring.

"WE HAVE STRUCK ICEBERG. SINKING FAST. COME TO OUR ASSISTANCE."

DISTRESS SIGNAL FROM THE *TITANIC*

The *Titanic* was the biggest ship afloat when it was launched.

The story of the *Titanic* has been told in many movies.

The key to the locker containing binoculars for the lookouts was missing from the ship. With binoculars, the lookouts might have seen the iceberg earlier, and the disaster could have been prevented.

EVERY MAN FOR HIMSELF

The iceberg had ripped open six compartments of the *Titanic*'s hull. Captain Smith knew that there were only enough lifeboats to save around half the people on the ship. The crew was ordered to evacuate women and children first, and many of the lifeboats were only half full when launched. As the front of the ship began to sink lower in the water, the captain told the radio operators to leave their posts, saying, "It's every man for himself."

Less than three hours after the collision, the *Titanic* disappeared beneath the waves. Hundreds of people were left in the icy sea, but they could not survive for long in the extreme cold.

AFTERMATH

More than 1,500 people lost their lives in the *Titanic* disaster. It is still the world's worst peacetime shipping disaster. In the years that followed, shipping law was changed so that ships had to carry enough lifeboats for all their passengers.

The *Titanic* would lie undisturbed at the bottom of the Atlantic Ocean for more than 70 years. Although many people suggested plans to recover the wreck, no one knew exactly where the wreck was.

EVA HART

Born: 1905

Died: 1996

Nationality: British

Titanic survivor Eva Hart was just seven years old when she traveled on the *Titanic* with her parents.

"AFTER THAT [THE SOUND OF STEAM ESCAPING] CAME THE WORST SOUND OF THE WHOLE DISASTER, WHICH WAS THE SOUND OF PEOPLE DROWNING, AND THAT'S SOMETHING THAT NO ONE COULD HEAR AND EVER FORGET."

EVA HART, *TITANIC* SURVIVOR

BENEATH THE WAVES

In the 1970s, a young ocean scientist named Robert Ballard started to make plans to find the *Titanic*. First, he tried lowering sonar equipment down to the seabed, but what he really needed was a mobile submarine that could work in the extreme cold and high pressure of the deep ocean.

The wreck of the *Titanic* is surrounded by a large area of debris that tells investigators more about the ship and how it sank.

The wreck of the *Titanic* lay on the seabed at a depth of almost 2.5 miles (4 kilometers).

ROBERT BALLARD

Born: 1942

Nationality: American

Although he was born far away from the sea in Wichita, Kansas, Robert Ballard made his name as one of the greatest explorers of shipwrecks and the ocean floor.

Exploring with *Argo*

Argo was attached to a surface ship and was equipped with sonar, cameras, and lights for scanning the seabed and sending back images from the pitch-black ocean depths. When *Argo* found something, the Jason module could be launched from it. This was fitted with thrusters, so it could move around objects and explore in more detail.

In 1985, Ballard returned to search for the ship using *Argo*, an unmanned underwater vehicle he had designed himself. For weeks, Ballard and his team scanned the seabed with sonar and *Argo*'s camera. Their expedition was about to return home when, on September 1, 1985, they found a large round object. It was one of the *Titanic*'s huge boilers. They had found the world's most famous shipwreck.

EXPLORING THE *TITANIC*

In 1986, Ballard and his team explored the wreck in a manned submersible named *Alvin*. The depth of the ocean meant that most of the team's time was spent traveling to and from the wreck. Over several dives, they explored the two parts of the wreck and the debris that littered the ocean floor. They even managed to send an unmanned module into the ship itself, down the huge first-class staircase!

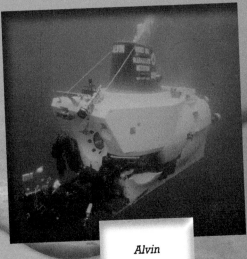

Alvin

SEARCHING FOR EVIDENCE

Since then, many expeditions have visited the wreck on the seabed. Scientists have found out much more about the fate of the *Titanic*. Evidence shows that rather than a single gash in the ship's side, the collision with the iceberg caused several small splits and damaged rivets holding the ship together.

In the 1950s, a plan suggested that the *Titanic* should be filled with ping-pong balls. Some people believed this would make it light enough to refloat, but the project would never have worked. In the deep ocean, ping-pong balls would have been crushed by the water pressure.

DAMAGING THE WRECK?

Each visit causes the ship to decay a bit more, as submersibles land on the wreck, disturb the water around it, and remove treasures. Experiments on the hull have found that the *Titanic* could have almost disappeared in another 100 years. Others disagree, arguing that we now have the technology to protect the ship for future generations to visit it on the ocean floor.

Some expeditions have recovered artifacts from the ship (such as this sink, above), and these have been sold at auction. Since 2012, 100 years after it sank, the ship has been protected by the International Convention on Underwater Cultural Heritage.

Exploring the *Titanic*

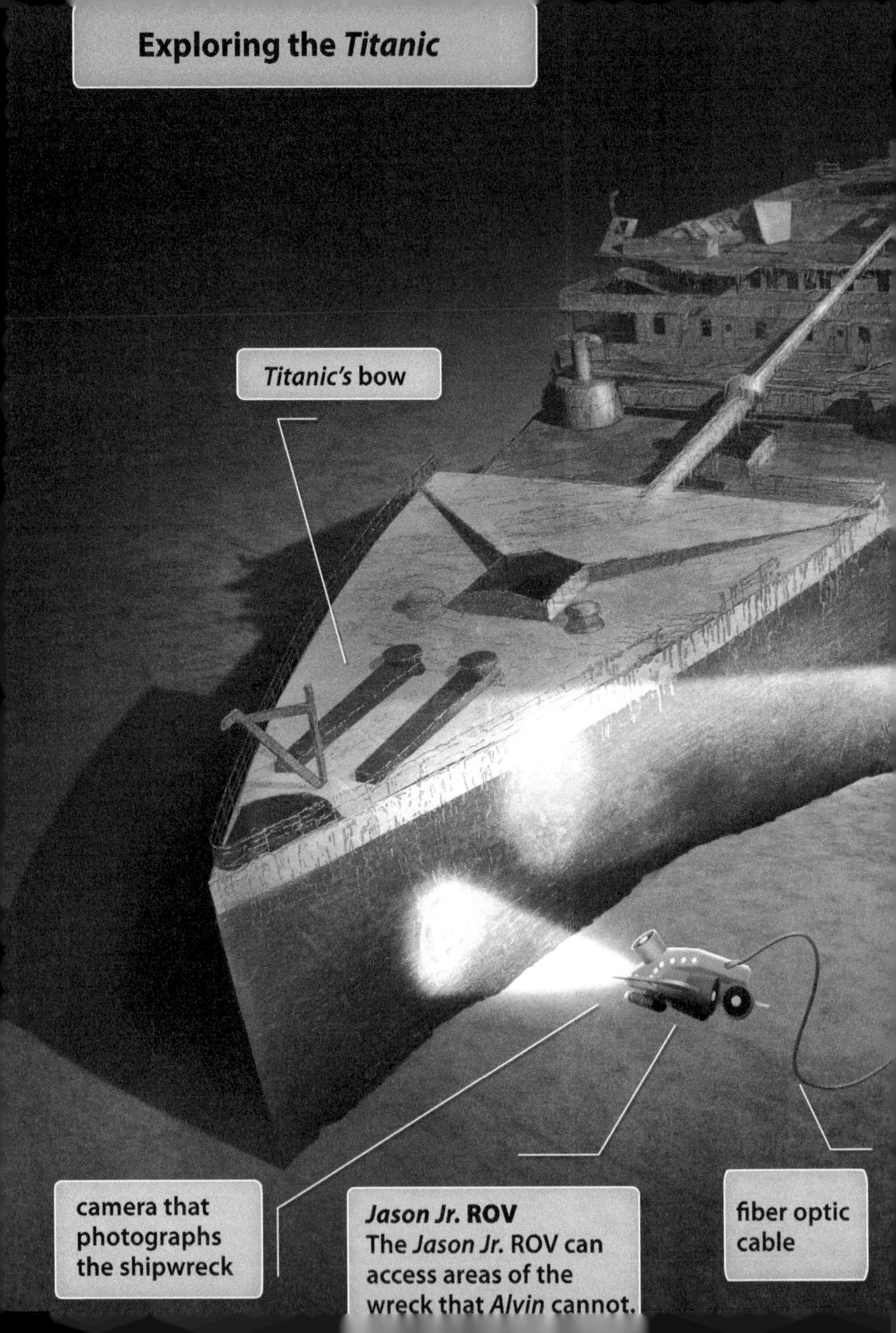

Titanic's bow

camera that photographs the shipwreck

Jason Jr. **ROV**
The *Jason Jr.* ROV can access areas of the wreck that *Alvin* cannot.

fiber optic cable

Titanic's stern

sonar

light

Alvin submersible
The lights on *Alvin* were needed to light up the gloom in the deep ocean.

ALVIN

cameras

crew inside *Alvin* remotely control *Jason Jr.*

TV camera

COULD YOU BE A MARITIME ARCHAEOLOGIST?

Some of the people who search for lost shipwrecks are maverick treasure hunters whose only interest is in finding gold and jewels that will make them rich. However, maritime archaeologists are attracted by shipwrecks because they help us learn about the past and because of the thrill of finding a wreck that has not been seen by anyone for hundreds of years.

Successful underwater archaeologists need lots of different skills. They need to be able to dive or use complex equipment to find wrecks beneath the ocean. If they need a reminder that the sea is a dangerous place to work, the wrecks themselves should serve as a warning.

To really understand historical shipwrecks, you need to learn about the history and archaeology of shipwrecks. Finding shipwrecks often means studying old maps and ships' documents. Most importantly, you must learn how to study a shipwreck without damaging it. If you can master all these skills, there may be a shipwreck out there waiting for you to discover it!

New shipwrecks are still being found. In 2011, a merchant ship from World War II (1939–1945) was discovered in the Atlantic Ocean with a cargo of more than 200 tons of silver. The ship was in an area of ocean even deeper than the *Titanic*, making it the deepest-ever treasure hunt.

Treasure technology

New technology has enabled treasure hunters to find shipwrecks in even the deepest oceans. Treasure can be salvaged without even diving to the wreck. Working with ROVs and computers has become an essential part of the treasure hunter's job.

TIMELINE

1545
The *Mary Rose* sinks when leaving harbor to do battle with a French fleet.

1622
Nuestra Señora de Atocha is wrecked in a storm while carrying cargo of silver and gold from the Americas to Spain.

1641
Merchant Royal is wrecked near Land's End in England, carrying one of the richest treasures of all time to the seabed.

1836
Diver John Deane discovers the wreck of the *Mary Rose* and salvages artifacts.

1865
The SS *Republic* sinks during a hurricane off the coast of Georgia.

1912
On April 14, the RMS *Titanic* hits an iceberg on its maiden voyage. The ship sinks in the early hours of April 15, claiming more than 1,500 lives.

1915
The ocean liner *Lusitania* is sunk by a German torpedo during World War I.

1942
Jacques-Yves Cousteau uses an Aqua-Lung for the first time and invents SCUBA diving.

1982
The *Mary Rose* is raised from the seabed on a giant floating crane. The ship is preserved in a specially built museum in Portsmouth, England.

1985
Robert Ballard's expedition finds the wreck of the *Titanic*.

Treasure hunter Mel Fisher and his team discover the main part of the treasure from *Nuestra Señora de Atocha*.

2001
The International Convention on Underwater Cultural Heritage agrees to protect shipwrecks from treasure hunters.

2003
Treasure hunters from Odyssey Marine Exploration discover the ship's bell that proves they have located the SS *Republic*.

GLOSSARY

Aqua-Lung tank containing compressed air that enables divers to breathe underwater

archaeologist person who studies the past by unearthing and examining historical remains

artifact anything made by humans, particularly something from the past

artillery large guns or cannon

Civil War in U.S. history, the conflict between two groups of states between 1861 and 1865 over the rights of 11 southern states to leave the union as well as the issue of slavery

colonial describing territory invaded or ruled over by another country—for example, as part of an empire. During the period 1584–1688, the eastern part of what is now the United States was ruled by Great Britain.

coral hard, rock-like, and often colorful substance made up of small marine mammals

corrode become damaged slowly by chemical action

debris wreckage or remains of something that has been destroyed or damaged

excavate dig up

fleet group of ships, such as a naval fleet going into battle

galleon large sailing ship, particularly used by the Spanish as warships and to transport treasure from the Americas

gun port opening in the side of a ship through which a cannon is fired

hurricane tropical storm with very strong swirling winds. In Asia, hurricanes are known as typhoons or cyclones.

ingot metal shaped into a bar so it can be stored or transported

knave old-fashioned word for a tricky person or villain

loot stolen goods

magnetometer piece of equipment that uses magnets to detect metals—for example, on the seabed

maiden voyage first official voyage taken by a ship

maverick outsider or independent person

ROV (remotely operated vehicle) unmanned vehicle that can be operated by remote control—for example, for exploring the deep ocean

salvage recover or repair, particularly relating to a sunken ship

SCUBA (self-contained underwater breathing apparatus) another word for Aqua-Lung

sonar using sound waves to detect or map something underwater

submersible vehicle that operates underwater

thruster type of engine that moves something by sending out a jet of air or water

torpedo missile fired from a submarine

wrecker person who lured ships onto the coast in order to loot them

FIND OUT MORE

BOOKS

Ballard, Robert. *Titanic: The Last Great Images*. Philadelphia: Running Press, 2008.

Ganeri, Anita. *The Sinking of the* Titanic *and Other Shipwrecks* (Incredible True Stories). New York: Rosen Central, 2012.

Platt, Richard, and Duncan Cameron. *Duncan Cameron's Shipwreck Detective*. New York: Dorling Kindersley, 2006.

Stewart, James. *Shipwrecks* (Amazing History). North Mankato, Minn.: Smart Apple Media, 2008.

WEB SITES

www.livescience.com/19633-6-deadliest-ocean-shipwrecks.html
This web site describes six of the deadliest shipwrecks of all time.

www.maryrose.org
Read the full story of the *Mary Rose* and the project to restore the ship.

odysseysvirtualmuseum.com/categories/SS-Republic
See artifacts from the SS *Republic* at this web site.

www.rmstitanic.net
Learn more about the *Titanic* at this web site.

www.shipwreck.net/ssrepublic.php
Find more information about the wreck and recovery of the SS *Republic*.

Places to Visit

Mel Fisher Maritime Heritage Society and Museum
200 Greene Street
Key West, Florida 33040
www.melfisher.org
This museum has a large collection of artifacts related to the *Atocha* shipwreck as well as other shipwrecks from the same period.

National Museum of the U.S. Navy
Washington Navy Yard
805 Kidder Breese Street SE
Washington, D.C. 20374-5060
www.history.navy.mil/branches/org8-1.htm
The National Museum of the U.S. Navy has a large collection of artifacts and other items related to the history of ships in the United States.

Titanic Museum Attraction
3235 76 Country Boulevard and Highway 165
Branson, Missouri 65616
www.titanicbranson.com
This museum contains many artifacts from the *Titanic* as well as interactive features such as a replica of the ship's grand staircase. The museum is shaped like the *Titanic*!

There are regular exhibitions of artifacts from the *Titanic* at museums around the world. There are also many maritime museums containing amazing stories and artifacts from shipwrecks. Check to see what exhibitions are near where you live.

Topics for Further Research

*   *Life on a warship in the 1500s*: Use what you have learned about the *Mary Rose* to find out more about life for sailors in the 1500s.

*   *Restoring the past*: How do archaeologists go about restoring artifacts from ancient shipwrecks, and why are they so opposed to commercial treasure hunting?

*   *Discover your own shipwreck*: This book has only explored a few of the thousands of shipwrecks around the world. Pick a shipwreck of your own to find out more about.

INDEX